M A K I N G
H E A L T H Y
F O O D
C H O I C E S

Special Diets and Food Allergies

Carol Ballard

www.heinemann.co.uk/library

Visit our website to find out more information about Heinemann Library books.

To order:

 Phone 44 (0) 1865 888066

 Send a fax to 44 (0) 1865 314091

 Visit the Heinemann Bookshop at www.heinemann.co.uk/library to browse our catalogue and order online.

First published in Great Britain by Heinemann Library, Halley Court, Jordan Hill, Oxford OX2 8EJ, part of Harcourt Education. Heinemann is a registered trademark of Harcourt Education Ltd.

Editorial: Andrew Farrow and
    Christine Mᶜ Cafferty
Design: David Poole and Geoff Ward
Illustrations: Geoff Ward
Picture Research: Melissa Allison and
    Maria Joannou
Production: Chloe Bloom

Originated by Chroma
Printed and bound in China by South China Printing Company

10 digit ISBN 0 431 11916 3 (hardback)
13 digit ISBN 978 0 431 11916 8
10 09 08 07 06
10 9 8 7 6 5 4 3 2 1

10 digit ISBN 0 431 11922 8 (paperback)
13 digit ISBN 978 0 431 11922 9
11 10 09 08 07
10 9 8 7 6 5 4 3 2 1

British Library Cataloguing in Publication Data
Ballard, Carol
Special diets and food allergies. - (Making healthy food choices)
613.2'6
A full catalogue record for this book is available from the British Library.

Acknowledgements
The publishers would like to thank the following for permission to reproduce photographs:
Alamy pp. 42 (Brand X Pictures), 50 (Paul Bradforth), 30 (Medical-on-Line); Anthony Blake Picture Library pp. 5 (Maximilian Stock Ltd), 39 (Joy Skipper), 40 (ATW Photography); Corbis pp. 7 (Brownie Harris), 8 (George Shelley), 15 (Tom Stewart), 17 (Cathrine Wessel), 19 (Najlah Feanny), 21 (Vittoriano Rastelli); Empics p. 12 (AP Photo/Domenico Stinellis); Getty Images pp. 20 (Photodisc), 29 (Iconica/ Raymond Patrick), 38 (Photodisc); Harcourt Education Ltd pp. 26 (MM Studios), 48 (MM Studios); istockphoto.com p. 51 (James McQuillan); Jupiterimages p. 46 (Photos.com); NASA p. 13); Photolibrary pp. 10 (Foodpix), 25 (Foodpix/John E Kelly), 44 (Workbook, Inc.); Rex Features pp. 18 (Burger /Phanie), 27 (GARO/Phanie), 36 (Garo / Phanie); Science Photo Library pp. 23 (BIOMEDICAL IMAGING UNIT, SOUTHAMPTON GENERAL HOSPITAL), 31 (AJ Photo), 35 (Paul Rapson), 37 (DR P. Marazzi), 41 (Ian Boddy).

Cover photograph of allergy test strips, reproduced with permission of Science Photo Library (Saturn Stills).

The publishers would like to thank Rebecca Weedon for her assistance in the preparation of this book.

The paper used to print this book comes from sustainable resources.

CONTENTS

Any words appearing in the text in bold, **like this**,
are explained in the glossary.

A HEALTHY DIET
– getting the right balance

Your diet is made up of everything you eat and everything you drink. This really does include everything – sweets, nibbles, and snacks as well as main meals! To keep you fit, healthy, and looking good, your diet must provide everything that your body needs.

A healthy diet should provide:
- enough energy for all your activities
- all the chemicals your body needs for growing and repairing itself
- other substances needed to maintain your general health.

It should not provide:
- a lot more energy than you use
- anything that might be harmful to your health.

HOW CAN YOU TELL IF YOUR DIET IS BALANCED?
To maintain a healthy diet you need to know what your body needs, and what food contains. The parts of food that our bodies can use are called **nutrients**. Different foods contain different nutrients. Some **dietitians** sort food into five main groups. Others put fruit and vegetables into two separate groups, making six groups in total. The six groups are:

- grains – such as bread, **cereals**, pasta, rice
- fruit – such as oranges, apples, strawberries, kiwis, bananas
- vegetables – such as broccoli, peas, carrots, lettuce, tomatoes
- dairy – such as milk, cheese, yoghurt
- meat, fish, eggs, nuts, beans – such as ham, turkey, tuna, baked beans, pine nuts
- fats, oils, sugars – such as olive oil, butter, cream, chocolate, sweets.

All the foods in a single food group contain similar nutrients. Your body needs more of some types of food than it does of others. Grains and starchy food should make up about a third of the food you eat. You should eat at least five portions of fruit and vegetables every day. Fruit and vegetables should make up a third of your food, although you can eat as much of them as you want. Raw fruits and vegetables usually contain more nutrients than cooked fruits and vegetables.

▲ This picture shows healthy foods that together can make a balanced diet.

Meat, fish, and eggs contain lots of **protein**, but you should not eat too much of them. They should make up about 10–15 per cent of your diet. High protein vegetarian alternatives are beans, nuts, and pulses. Try not to consume too much milk or dairy. Two to three servings (about 15 per cent) a day is enough. There are soya alternatives for vegetarians.

Make sure that you do not eat too much oil, fat, or sugar. These should make up less than 10 per cent of your diet. The group includes cakes, crisps, and soft drinks. High salt foods can also be included in this group.

Why each food group is good for you

food group	good source of	needed for
cereals	starch, fibre	energy, keeping digestive system working smoothly
vegetables	vitamins, minerals, fibre	general health, keeping digestive system working smoothly
fruit	vitamins, minerals, fibre	general health, keeping digestive system working smoothly
meat, fish, eggs, nuts, beans	proteins	growth and repairing damage
dairy	minerals especially calcium	strong bones and teeth
fats, oils, and sweets	fats and sugars	energy

WATER MATTERS!

Water is another important part of the human diet. Many foods include some water, but to get enough water we also need to drink. Taking in too little water can lead to **dehydration**. This can make you feel ill, and at worst can be dangerous. You need extra water or other fluids in hot weather, and when you are taking part in sports and other physical activities.

DIFFERENT PEOPLE, DIFFERENT NEEDS

A **balanced diet** is ideal for most healthy people who do an average amount of physical activity. However, it does not suit everybody – some people need a special diet.

A special diet is one that is significantly different in some way from a normal, balanced diet. Some special diets include different amounts of a particular type of food. Others completely exclude a particular food or food group. Some special diets provide extra energy, or extra amounts of a particular nutrient.

WHO MIGHT NEED A SPECIAL DIET?

All sorts of different people need a special diet, for a wide variety of reasons. These reasons include:

- Medical conditions: In some medical conditions, such as allergies, the body reacts badly to particular foods, so these need to be excluded from the diet. In other medical conditions, the body may need more of a particular nutrient or food group than a balanced diet would provide.

- Physical activities: Sports and other physical activities make extra demands on a person's body. To be able to meet these demands, the diet may need to provide more energy, and in some cases extra nutrients, than a balanced diet would provide.

- Special conditions: Under different environmental conditions, a balanced diet may not be suitable. For example, people living and working in polar or desert regions, and people living and working in areas where there has been a famine would have different requirements than a normal balanced diet would provide.

We all have foods that we dislike, but you cannot simply say you're on a special diet to avoid them! Leaving out something may unbalance your diet and affect your health.

Detox diets

Detox is short for detoxification, which means to get rid of poisons. This is what a detox, or cleansing, diet is supposed to do. Some people choose to follow a diet like this for a short period, often after a holiday or long celebration. Detox diets usually contain only raw vegetables, fresh fruit, water, and yoghurt. Many people say they feel much better after living on a restricted diet like this for a week.

However, detox diets have not been scientifically proven to be beneficial. Many doctors feel they do not provide all the nutrients the body needs. This sort of diet is definitely not recommended for young people. As they are still growing, young people in particular need a proper balance of nutrients in their food.

MEDICAL ADVICE NEEDED

You should ask your doctor before going on a special diet. A doctor's or dietitian's expert knowledge can help to make sure that the special diet will provide your body with all the nutrients it needs.

▲ People are different in many ways, but we all need a balanced diet in order to be healthy.

FOOD FOR ALL STAGES OF LIFE

At different stages in our lives, our bodies grow, change, and mature. Sometimes we take part in different everyday activities. This means that parts of our diets may need to change too, to match our physical and lifestyle changes.

BABIES AND TODDLERS

At first, milk provides newborn babies with all the energy and nutrients that they need to grow and develop. Some mothers breastfeed their babies using milk from their own bodies. Other mothers use a special milky mixture, sometimes called a formula, which they feed from a bottle.

A few months after birth, a baby begins to need more solid food to help it grow. At first babies have no teeth, so they can only manage soft, mushy food. Gradually, they are able to eat harder and more varied foods. Just like an adult, a toddler needs a balanced diet, but as their bodies are so much smaller, the actual amounts of nutrients and energy needed are smaller too.

▲ This man and his grandchild have different nutritional needs because they are at different stages of their life.

CHILDHOOD AND ADOLESCENCE

Children grow very rapidly and are usually very active – their games often involve a lot of running around! They need a balanced diet that provides plenty of energy. This allows their bodies to grow and develop fully, and to be as active as they wish. Children who are less active need less energy from their food.

The years between childhood and adulthood are called adolescence. During these teenage years, the body matures and grows. Body shape changes too. For example, a boy's shoulders broaden and a girl's hips widen. Teenagers can be very active, too, taking part in many activities such as team games, athletics, dancing, cycling, and swimming. During adolescence, eating a balanced diet will provide enough nutrients for growth and development, and lots of energy too!

ADULTHOOD AND OLD AGE

By the end of adolescence, the body is fully mature and has reached its full height. No more growth will take place, although bones continue to strengthen until the mid-twenties. A normal balanced diet will fulfil the needs of most adults. Throughout adulthood, it is important to continue to match the energy provided by food to level of activity.

People are often less active when they are old than they were when they were younger, so their energy needs may be reduced. However, it is still important that their diet provides a full range of nutrients in order to maintain general health and fitness.

Nutrition during pregnancy

✔ Before its birth, a baby receives all its **nutrition** from its mother. Her diet must therefore supply all the energy and nutrients for them both.

✔ People often talk about "eating for two", but this doesn't really mean the mother needs to eat twice as much of everything! Instead, a balanced diet, with extra amounts of some nutrients such as iron, calcium, and fibre will keep both mother and baby healthy.

✔ **Folic acid**, before and during pregnancy, is particularly important to prevent conditions such as **spina bifida** in the baby. In many parts of the world, folic acid supplements are recommended. In the US, folic acid is added to many foods during the production process.

DIET AND CHOICE ?
– how do you choose

We each have our own favourite foods and own particular foods that we dislike. Our food choices are influenced by these preferences. Most people also make other choices about the foods they eat, for many different reasons.

As well as choosing foods we like and avoiding foods that we do not, we also make food choices for a variety of other reasons. Ethical, religious, cultural, geographical, and financial factors can all influence our personal food choices.

▲ Vegetarians, people who don't eat meat, can still enjoy a healthy and varied diet.

ETHICS AND FOOD CHOICES

People may choose to avoid some types of food because they think it is morally wrong to eat it. Some people are vegetarian because they think it is wrong to eat meat. Others eat meat only from **free range** animals, as they are concerned about animal welfare issues. Environmental concerns, such as the pollution that is caused by transporting food over long distances, means some people prefer to buy local produce. Many people choose foods produced under "fair trade" agreements because they are concerned about the pay and conditions of agricultural workers.

RELIGION AND FOOD CHOICES

Some religions have rules or traditions about what followers may and may not eat. Sometimes these apply only to particular periods in the year. For example, Muslims must not eat or drink during daylight hours during Ramadan. Other religious rules apply all the time, so Hindus and Buddhists follow a vegetarian diet. Some religious rules apply to the way food is prepared or stored, such as Islamic **halal meat** and Jewish **kosher** foods.

CULTURES AND FOOD CHOICES

Different cultures have developed customs and habits that can affect food choices. Many people make the traditional choices that are the norm within their culture. Such choices often appear strange to people from other cultures – for example, eating raw fish for breakfast in America might seem unusual, but in Japan it is common. Eating worms might seem strange to people in Europe, but in some parts of Southern Africa mopane worms are an important part of the people's diet. They are very high in protein.

GEOGRAPHY AND FOOD CHOICES

Foods that grow easily in a particular area are cheaper and more plentiful than those that do not. People have therefore traditionally eaten their local foods. They also ate what was in season at different times of the year.

Wheat grows well and is plentiful in Europe. There the traditional starchy foods are made from wheat flour, such as bread and pasta. In Asia, rice is grown instead of wheat, so the traditional starchy foods of Asia are made from rice and rice-based foods.

In recent years people's food choices have become much wider, as modern transport and food preservation methods make it easier to obtain food from distant places. Also people no longer have to eat food only when it is in season.

FINANCE AND FOOD CHOICES

The price of different foods may influence our food choices. Some people may not be able to afford expensive foods and others may choose not to buy them. On special occasions, such as birthdays and other celebrations, people often choose to spend more than usual on food. Buying luxury foods is all part of the celebration.

OUT OF THE ORDINARY!

A balanced diet usually provides all the energy and nutrients for normal, everyday living. However, taking part in special activities, or living in unusual conditions, may mean that the body needs a different balance of nutrients, and more or less energy than usual.

SPORTS, EXERCISE, AND DIET

Sporting activities use more energy than just sitting down or walking around slowly. This means that most people who do regular sports need more **calories** than those who do not. Many serious sportspeople follow carefully planned diets that ensure their food provides the right amount of energy and a good balance of nutrients.

Sports dietitians are qualified to provide advice about sports and diet. General tips that are good for anyone doing sport include:

- eat a balanced diet, with plenty of **carbohydrates**
- eat regular meals – do not skip breakfast
- eat a meal about two hours before exercise, then a carbohydrate-rich snack about five minutes before exercise
- drink water or sports drinks while exercising to combat dehydration and to maintain your energy
- make sure your diet provides enough iron and calcium (to prevent **anaemia** and fatigue).

▶ A banana will provide this tennis player with extra energy, vitamins, and minerals.

▲ Food used in space must be light-weight and compact. It must not leave crumbs.

NUTRITION IN SPACE

In space, astronauts need similar nutrients to those needed on Earth, but their diet usually has slightly less fat and fibre and slightly more carbohydrate than a normal diet. Being weightless for long periods can weaken bones. To maintain bone strength, astronauts need plenty of calcium in their diet, along with some extra vitamins. For practical reasons, some other factors are also important. Food for astronauts must:

* be able to be stored for long periods
* contain no **microbes** such as bacteria
* create minimal waste.

NUTRITION IN POLAR REGIONS

Because of the extreme cold and their high levels of physical activity, people who live and work in polar regions use a lot more energy than normal. On average, they need a diet that provides 5,000–6,000 calories per day   more than twice as much as they would need in a warmer climate. Eating extra carbohydrate or fat can provide this energy.

NUTRITION AFTER FAMINE

After famines, many people, especially children, suffer from lack of protein and energy. Their muscles are wasted, they have no stored fat, and the shapes of their bones can be seen through their loose skin. Such people urgently need food, but their diet must be very carefully controlled. Their livers and **intestines** often do not function normally so they cannot cope with normal amounts of protein, fat, and salt. A liquid mixture made from dried skimmed milk, sugar, cereal flour, oil, minerals, and vitamins must be given in small quantities every few hours. Once normal body functions are restored, usually after three to seven days, solid food can slowly be reintroduced.

DIET AND WEIGHT CONTROL
– a balancing act

Balancing the energy you take in and the energy you use is the key to controlling your body weight. Taking in more energy than you use will lead to an increase in weight. Taking in less energy than you use will lead to a decrease in weight.

Most people find a comfortable balance between the amount of energy their food provides and the amount of energy they use up in their everyday activities. This is ideal – their lifestyle and diet are balanced and stable.

STAYING STABLE

If your food provides more energy than you use in your everyday activities, your body stores the extra energy. It does not make any difference whether you take in the extra energy as carbohydrate, protein, or fat. The body digests the food into its separate chemicals and releases the energy the food contains. Some energy is used for vital processes and activities. Any extra energy is then stored as fat inside special fat cells. Together, lots of fat cells make a material called adipose tissue. This collects in the abdomen, around organs, and under the skin.

If your food provides less energy than you use in your everyday activities, you lose weight. This is because your body has to use up some of its energy stores. The fat stored in adipose tissue is broken down into separate chemicals. This breaking-down process releases energy. As your stored fat is used up, you lose weight.

What does it take?	
activity	approximate calories used per hour
watching television	60
walking	210
badminton	220
weight-training	260
dancing	280
kayaking	352
cycling	360
aerobics	400
skiing	422
tennis	440
basketball	460
ice skating	493
swimming	520
running	580
beach volleyball	563

▲ Too many snacks and too little exercise can lead to a weight increase!

FINDING A BALANCE

Your body uses energy even when you are asleep, because vital processes such as breathing, pumping blood around the body, and digesting food must continue all the time. These basic processes use up energy at a steady rate whatever you are doing. The actual amount they use is different from person to person, and is affected by your gender, age, height, weight, and race. An average adult uses about 1.1 kcal every minute – or nearly 1,600 kcal every day – just to stay alive!

Everything you do uses up extra energy. Some activities use up a lot more energy than others. Knowing how much extra energy your activities use up can help you to keep a check on whether your food provides about the right amount of energy, too much, or too little.

You need to find the balance that is right for your age and gender. However, most young people find that if they keep active and eat a healthy, balanced diet, their body will naturally keep the right balance.

WHY LOSE WEIGHT?

Being **obese** is not good for your health. It can also make sports and ordinary everyday activities difficult. There are three main reasons for wanting to lose weight:

1. Being obese makes it harder for your body to work efficiently. Your heart has to work harder to pump blood around. You become out of breath more quickly. Your muscles have to work harder to move the extra weight. Joints such as your knees are under greater strain supporting the extra weight.

2. Being obese can make everyday activities difficult. Things that should be enjoyable, such as sport and dancing, are much less fun when they feel like hard work. Jobs such as housework, shopping, and gardening all become harder too. Even sitting in a cinema seat can be awkward if the seat is too small.

3. Many people also think that being slim is more attractive than being obese.

WHAT IS AN IDEAL WEIGHT?

Because everybody is different, there is no standard measurement that can tell you exactly what you should weigh. Many doctors use a scale called BMI (Body Mass Index) which links weight and height.

An adult person's BMI is calculated by dividing their weight by the square of their height. This results in a figure, which can be compared with this scale:

- less than 17.5 = underweight
- 17.5–24.9 = normal range
- 25–29.9 = overweight
- 30+ = obese

A person who is 1.6 metres (5.2 feet) tall and weighs 55 kilograms (120 pounds) has a BMI of 21.5. This falls within the normal range. There are many calculators on the Internet that you can use to calculate your BMI.

Generally, a person with a BMI greater than 30 is considered obese. However, these figures can be misleading because muscle weighs more than fat. This means that people with powerful muscles, such as rowers, rugby players, and American football players could easily have a BMI between 25 and 30. According to their BMI scores they are overweight, but this is due to the amount of muscle in their bodies.

SAFE WEIGHT LOSS

Most doctors recommend that to lose weight safely you should still eat a balanced diet, but reduce your energy intake. Losing weight is a big commitment, but for most people a safe weight loss is 0.5–1 kilograms (1.1–2.2 pounds) per week. One kilogram (2.2 pounds) of fat contains about 7,000 kcal. If you eat around 3,500 calories (kcal) less than your body uses each week, you will lose 0.5 kilograms (1.1 pounds). If you also increase your activity levels and burn an extra 3,500 calories each week, you only need to reduce your energy intake by 3,500 calories and you will achieve your 1 kilogram (2.2 pound) weight loss!

FAD DIETS

There are some weird diets around! Some suggest eating just one type of food, while others ban a particular food group. From a health point of view, they can be really bad news. They do not provide a full balance of the nutrients your body needs to stay fit and healthy. Some provide so little energy that you feel tired all the time and are unable to concentrate properly. Diets like this may promise rapid weight loss. As soon as you go back to eating normally though, the weight often comes straight back. However overweight you are, your body still needs its full range of nutrients – and that means a balanced diet.

◄ Taking part in sport like this can be great fun – and it burns up plenty of energy!

GAINING WEIGHT – HOW AND WHY?

Being underweight can be just as much of a problem as being overweight. Some people need to gain weight in order to be fit and healthy.

Being underweight is not good for your body. If you eat too little, your body will not have enough nutrients and energy, and may not be able to grow and develop properly. Vital organs may be weakened, and this will affect your general health. Weak muscles and bones make it difficult to be active and carry out ordinary everyday tasks. Your **immune system** may also be weakened, so that you are less able to fight off germs and infections. Also, some people think that being underweight is unattractive.

There are several reasons why a person might be underweight. There are some medical conditions where the body cannot tolerate, process, or use particular foods. Long periods of illness can also result in a slow weight loss. Some people may over-exercise or follow a slimming diet excessively so they lose too much weight. Eating disorders such as anorexia nervosa can also result in severe weight loss.

Elderly people often find it difficult to maintain a normal body weight, too. This may be because they have difficulty eating, or have less appetite, and so do not eat enough. Also, because of illness, some may need more energy than they would if they were well.

▼ After an illness, patients often need to regain weight they have lost.

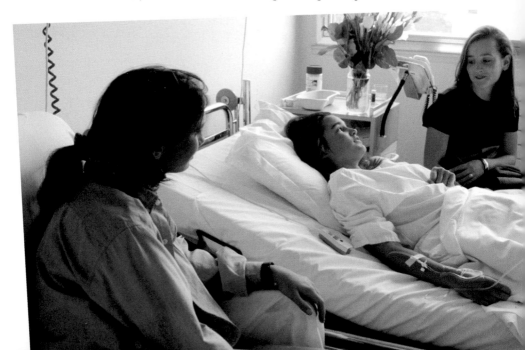

▲ Many people buy supplements for building muscles, but the same results can be achieved in a healthier way by eating the right foods.

SAFE WEIGHT GAIN

Energy-rich foods, such as chocolate, can help a person to gain weight. However, it is important not to obtain all the additional energy from fats and sugars. A general guide to gaining weight safely is to increase body muscle rather than body fat. Eating regular protein-rich and starch-rich meals, with nutritious snacks between, will help to build muscle mass. Useful tips include adding extras to an ordinary meal, for example by adding grated cheese to pasta dishes, and snacking on foods such as dried fruit. Although the precise diet may vary for people with particular medical conditions, for most healthy people weight gain is best achieved by following the guidelines for a normal balanced diet.

It is also important to take in plenty of vitamins and minerals, especially calcium for strong teeth and bones and general health. Dairy products, such as custard, milk puddings and porridge (with milk), are often invaluable for elderly people and those recovering from illness. Some special liquid foods are also available to help patients gain weight lost through age or illness.

WEIGHT GAIN SUPPLEMENTS

Some people buy protein supplements to help them build muscle mass. In general, though, it is better to get all the nutrition you need from a normal diet.

DIET AND MEDICAL CONDITIONS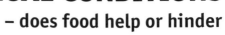
– does food help or hinder

There are many medical conditions for which people are advised to follow special dietary guidelines. In some conditions, the consequences of ignoring such advice can be relatively minor. In others, though, failure to follow the guidelines can be life-threatening.

Diet can affect every part of the body and therefore it can affect medical conditions of every body system. Examples of medical conditions that can be affected by diet include:

- digestive system problems, such as **coeliac disease** and bowel cancer
- heart and circulation problems
- kidney disease

- cystic fibrosis
- **diabetes**
- **migraine**, **eczema**, and **asthma**
- gout and **arthritis**.

▲ Foods such as raw fish and seaweed, as found in a traditional Japanese diet, may provide protection against some bowel disorders.

HOW CAN DIET AFFECT MEDICAL CONDITIONS?

There are several ways that diet can affect medical conditions.

- Accumulation of substances from the food. For example, a build-up of fatty substances in arteries can cause problems with blood circulation and heart disease.
- Lack of a particular substance. This can occur when the body needs more of a substance than normal. For example, a person suffering from iron deficiency anaemia needs additional iron in their diet. Without it, the anaemia will worsen or not improve, making them feel tired and lethargic.

▲ Using oil from olives like these, instead of animal fats, can help to keep the heart and blood vessels healthy.

- Eating a prohibited or trigger food. This can make a condition worse, or can cause a dormant condition to reappear. For example, some migraine sufferers can avoid a migraine attack by following a cheese-free diet, but as soon as they eat cheese, an attack will be triggered.
- Getting the balance wrong. In some medical conditions, the levels of certain substances in the body are finely balanced. Upsetting this balance can cause a worsening of the condition. For example, patients with some forms of kidney disease have to monitor and control their intake of potassium and water very carefully.
- Eating at the right time. Timing when food is eaten can be important. For example, many patients with diabetes need to eat regularly. They need carbohydrates at each meal, and may need additional snacks as well.

FOLLOWING DIETARY ADVICE

For many people who have to live with a medical condition, managing their diet becomes automatic. Initially, a doctor or dietitian will give information and advice. This usually involves explaining how diet and the person's medical condition are linked, and what effects any dietary changes may have on their health. Fact sheets, diet sheets, and menu plans can help the patient to get used to their new eating plan.

PROCESSING YOUR FOOD

Everything that you eat and drink passes through your digestive system. You can think of your digestive system as a long, continuous tube. Food goes into your mouth. As food travels through the digestive system, it is broken down, nutrients are absorbed and waste leaves your body via the anus. A diet that contains plenty of fibre can help to keep food moving easily through the digestive system.

DIVERTICULOSIS AND DIVERTICULITIS

If the walls of the large intestine become weak, small pouches can form. This is called diverticulosis and usually causes no problems. However, if the pouches become **inflamed**, the condition is called diverticulitis. This can cause pain and prevent the large intestine from working normally. Eating plenty of fresh fruit, vegetables, and wholegrain food can ease the symptoms and help the digestive system to recover. People who have had diverticulitis are often advised to switch to a high-fibre diet.

CROHN'S DISEASE

In people with Crohn's disease, parts of the bowel become inflamed and **ulcerated**. This usually occurs in patches, but can occur anywhere from the mouth to the anus. Its symptoms include **diarrhoea** or **constipation**, **malabsorption**, abdominal pain, tiredness, and weight loss. Dietary advice may be to eat high-calorie, high-protein foods to replace energy and nutrients. A low-fibre, low-fat diet can help to reduce flare ups. Extra liquids need to be drunk to avoid dehydration. Small, frequent meals with snacks in between may be better than three meals a day. Sometimes, the gut needs a complete rest to allow some healing to take place. The patient is given special foods, rather than eating or drinking normal foods. Sometimes these have to be given via a tube that leads from the nose to the stomach.

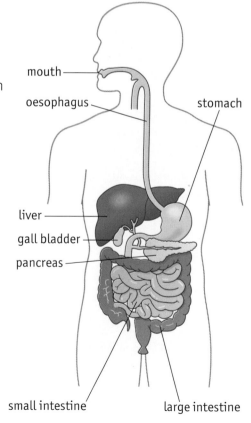

mouth

oesophagus

stomach

liver

gall bladder

pancreas

small intestine

large intestine

▲ Your diet can have a significant effect on your digestive system and how it functions.

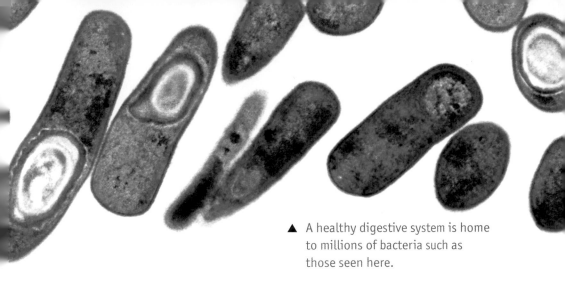

▲ A healthy digestive system is home to millions of bacteria such as those seen here.

COELIAC DISEASE

People with coeliac disease are sensitive to **gluten**. This is a protein found in cereals such as wheat, rye, and barley. In these people, gluten causes bowel inflammation that prevents their digestive system absorbing nutrients properly. They may lose weight and have problems, such as anaemia, due to lack of vitamins. If gluten is completely removed from their diet, the symptoms disappear and the patient recovers. However, they then need to keep to a gluten-free diet for life.

IRRITABLE BOWEL SYNDROME

Irritable bowel syndrome (IBS) affects a large number of people. It makes them feel bloated and uncomfortable, with frequent abdominal cramps. It can also cause diarrhoea and constipation. IBS may arise after another illness, or stress. However, the symptoms can be caused by many different problems; only a doctor can diagnose IBS.

Many patients with IBS are advised to eat a normal balanced diet, but to avoid caffeine, high-fat, and spicy foods. Some people find foods such as live yoghurt help, but for others these foods have the opposite effect. IBS can affect people in different ways, and so dietary advice will differ from one patient to another.

BACTERIA

Millions of bacteria live in your large intestine! They do an important job, keeping the gut healthy – but they also produce gas. In some IBS sufferers, the gas causes an unpleasant bloated feeling – as well as embarrassing flatulence!

HOW CAN FOOD HELP THE HEART AND LUNGS?

Without an efficient blood circulation and oxygen intake, your body will not be fit and healthy – so your diet needs to help to keep these systems in tip-top condition. There are three main parts of the circulatory system:

1. the heart, which pumps blood
2. the blood vessels, through which blood travels
3. the blood itself.

The heart is a muscle and needs nutrients just like the rest of your muscles. Scientific evidence shows that eating a balanced diet can help to keep a heart healthy and strong. This means eating plenty of protein, vitamins, and minerals, as well as carbohydrates. Many people who have heart disease actually have problems with the blood vessels that go to and from the heart, rather than with the heart itself.

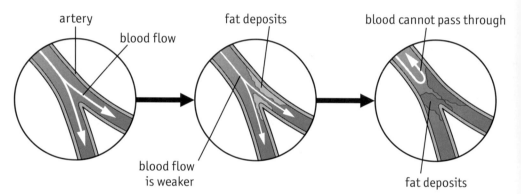

▲ Blood vessels can become blocked by fats that travel around in the blood.

DIET AND BLOOD VESSELS

Arteries, veins, and capillaries form a network of vessels that carry blood around to every part of your body. Blockages due to a build-up of fats in a major vessel, such as those supplying the heart muscle itself, can be very dangerous.

Measuring the amount of **cholesterol** in the blood can help show whether blood vessels are getting clogged up. People with high cholesterol levels, or those who already have heart disease or narrowed blood vessels, are usually advised to avoid foods that contain **saturated fats**. This reduces the chances of any further fat being deposited in the blood vessels. Eating **unsaturated fats**, such as those found in fish oils, can protect the vessels from becoming blocked. **Antioxidants** are chemicals found in many fruits and vegetables. They have also been found to have a protective effect.

DIET AND BLOOD

Red blood cells carry oxygen around the body. To do this, they need iron. Without enough iron the cells carry less oxygen and you feel tired and lethargic. This is known as iron-deficiency anaemia. People who suffer from this condition need to eat iron-rich foods, such as liver, eggs, beans, nuts, and cereals.

DIET AND LUNGS: CYSTIC FIBROSIS

Most people have healthy lungs, so they take in oxygen efficiently. This is not the case for people with the genetic condition called cystic fibrosis. The balance of salt and water in the body is upset and a thick mucus is produced. This clogs up the lungs and leads to breathing problems and chest infections. It also prevents the intestines from absorbing fats and vitamins properly. Because of this, people with cystic fibrosis need to include more fat in their diet than healthy people. A high-calorie diet, often with regular, high-energy snacks, and vitamin supplements, is often recommended.

▶ Eating plenty of fruit can help to keep your heart and blood vessels healthy.

WHAT IS THE LINK BETWEEN DIET AND DIABETES?

Diabetes affects the way your body handles sugar. This means that diabetics have to be very careful about what they eat and when they eat it.

In people with diabetes, the body's system for controlling the amount of sugar in the blood does not function properly. When sugars and starchy foods are eaten, they are converted into glucose, a type of sugar that can be used as an energy source. Glucose is transported around the body in the blood, to places where energy is needed. The level of sugar in the blood is carefully controlled by a balance of two **hormones** produced by the pancreas:

- **insulin**: if the blood-sugar level rises, insulin is released, making the liver remove glucose from the blood and store it.

- **glucagon**: if the blood-sugar level drops, glucagon is released, making the liver release stored glucose into the blood.

In people with diabetes, the insulin system does not work properly. This means that excess sugar builds up in the blood.

▼ Sugar-free foods like these should still only be eaten in small quantities.

Different types of diabetes

✔ Type I diabetes usually starts in childhood. The pancreas does not produce enough insulin.

✔ Type II diabetes mainly used to affect people over the age of 30 but in recent years it has also begun to affect a significant number of younger people. The pancreas produces some insulin but the body is often less responsive to it. This condition is called "insulin resistance".

CONTROLLING DIABETES

As a diabetic's blood-sugar control system does not work properly, the person has to control it themselves. To do this, Type I diabetics need to inject themselves with insulin regularly. They have to pay careful attention to their diet. It is important that meals are eaten at regular times. Also, the amount and type of food eaten must be balanced with the amount of physical activity. A normal balanced diet is recommended for most diabetics. This is important in order to prevent complications. For example, people with diabetes are at higher risk of heart disease.

LIFE WITHOUT SUGAR?

In the past, diabetics were usually advised to eat no sugar at all. This was often difficult and boring – just imagine never being able to eat any of your favourite sugary treats! Sugar free foods, made using artificial sweeteners

▲ This girl is diabetic and needs to inject herself regularly with insulin.

instead of sugar, were developed. Jams, jellies, biscuits, sweets, and chocolates made for diabetics were very expensive, but made life more enjoyable. Although these foods are still available, they are much less important now than in the past. This is because diabetics are no longer told they need to avoid sugar. A low-sugar diet is recommended for both diabetics and non-diabetics.

CAN FOOD CAUSE MIGRAINES?

Many people use the word migraine to describe a bad headache, but a real migraine is much more than just a headache. Although factors such as stress and hormone fluctuations are responsible for migraine attacks in some people, diet can also play a part.

A migraine involves the blood vessels within the brain. They widen and narrow, affecting blood flow in and around the brain. This altered blood flow affects nerves close by, and causes a wide range of symptoms. There may be early warning signs that a migraine is about to begin, such as flashing lights or a particular smell or taste.

Once the migraine really begins, it can cause sickness and diarrhoea, dizziness, sensitivity to light, distorted vision – and a really terrible headache. Strangely, in many people the migraine is restricted to just one side of the head and body. Typically, a migraine attack can last from several hours to three or four days.

A recent survey by the American Council for Headache Education (ACHE) has found that migraines are far more common in school-age children than many believe. Some school nurses have reported that they see more than ten students a month for headaches, many of which may be migraines. Serious migraines affect a young person's ability to function in school.

There are a number of ways to recognize migraines, including:

- awakening from sleep due to a headache
- worsening or more frequent headaches
- early morning vomiting without nausea
- fever or a stiff neck.

HOW DOES DIET AFFECT MIGRAINES?

For some migraine sufferers, their attacks are closely linked to what they eat and drink. Keeping a food diary can help them to link their attacks to particular foods. The attack may follow immediately or there may be a time lag of a day or so.

Common triggers include chocolate, alcohol, caffeine, citrus fruits, cheese, and artificial sweeteners. Once the trigger foods have been identified and excluded from the diet, sufferers can stay free of migraines for years.

▲ This man is suffering the headache and sickness of a migraine.

A MIGRAINE SUFFERER SAYS:

"My first warning that a migraine is about to hit me is a horrible taste of metal polish in my mouth. If I take my medicine at that point, I can reduce the severity of the attack, but I can't stop it completely. I need to get home and lie down as quickly as possible because within a couple of hours I'll be so dizzy, wobbly, and sick that I won't be able to stand up without falling over. I'll be flat out in bed for a couple of days and then still feel rough for a day or so after that. My head feels like there's a red hot knife slicing it in two, my eyes won't focus properly, lights flash, all the left side of my body tingles, and I'm usually very, very sick.

One of my worst trigger foods is cheese. I used to love Italian food, especially pizza, but since I worked out what my trigger foods were, I never risk eating cheese. A migraine makes me feel so awful that now I'd rather go hungry than feel that ill. Another bad one for me is aspartame – an artificial sweetener found in fizzy drinks. It's all right if I just have a little, but I can't drink too much or I'll feel the warning signs and know I need to stop."

Carrie

ECZEMA AND ASTHMA – IS FOOD INVOLVED?

Eczema and asthma are becoming more common than they used to be. This may in part be due to chemicals and other environmental factors, but for many people their diet may also play a part.

Eczema is a condition that affects the skin. It is often worse around joints such as elbows, wrists, and knees but it can affect the skin anywhere on the body. The skin becomes dry, flaky, and itchy. Scratching the itching skin can then make things worse by leading to bleeding and infection.

Illness, stress, anxiety, and contact with chemicals can all trigger eczema. In many people, it can also be triggered by certain foods. Not eating a particular food may help the condition improve. Scientists have found that in children with eczema, the intestines may not absorb food in the normal way. Children's eczema is often associated with food, but they may later grow out of it.

WHICH FOODS CAN TRIGGER ECZEMA?

Just about any food is a potential eczema trigger, but some are more commonly involved than others. Cows' milk, eggs, soya, wheat, fish, and nuts have all been shown to trigger eczema in some people. Eliminating these foods from the diet is unlikely to cure the eczema completely, but may help to reduce its effects. However, sufferers should talk to a doctor before trying this as a treatment method.

▼ Here you can see the red, itchy skin on the hand of a person with eczema.

▲ Many asthma sufferers need an inhaler to help them to breathe easily.

WHAT IS ASTHMA?

Asthma affects the tiny airways in the lungs. In response to a particular trigger, the airways tighten and narrow, making breathing difficult. Inflammation may follow, along with production of sticky mucus that clogs the airways even more.

Many things in the environment can trigger an asthma attack, such as dust, pollen, pets, air pollutants – and some foods. Restricting or avoiding trigger foods cannot usually cure a person's asthma. Unless a doctor advises differently, they will need to keep taking their medication as normal. However, keeping a food diary can help to identify particular foods that make the asthma worse. Foods commonly associated with asthma include cows' milk, eggs, fish, shellfish, yeast, nuts, and some food additives. Herbal remedies and other complementary medicines should only be taken after medical advice as some, such as echinacea and royal jelly, can be particularly dangerous for asthmatics.

WHAT IS AN ALLERGY?
– the body's response

Some people are **allergic** to a particular food or food group. You probably know that this means they should not eat those foods. However, do you know why? What really happens when someone eats a food to which they are allergic?

Allergies, **allergens**, and allergic responses – all these words can be confusing! If you have an allergy to a substance, you are said to be allergic to it. The substance itself is called an allergen. When your body is exposed to the allergen, your body reacts to it and you suffer an allergic response. Some allergic responses occur when the person touches or breathes in the allergen. To suffer an allergic response to food, you usually have to swallow the food. In some severe cases, though, just letting it touch your lips is enough to trigger an allergic response.

HOW DOES THE BODY RESPOND TO AN ALLERGEN?

When you eat a food to which you are allergic, your body's defence mechanisms swing into action. These defence mechanisms are part of your body's immune system, which protects you from germs and diseases.

First time allergen enters body:

Next time allergen enters body:

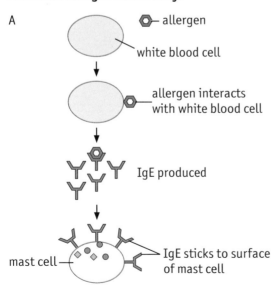

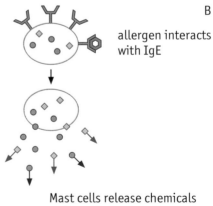

Mast cells release chemicals such as histamine. These circulate in the blood and cause symptoms of the allergic response such as skin rash.

▲ (A) shows how an allergic response develops. There has been no allergic response yet, but the system is primed and ready.
(B) is when the allergen next enters the body and there is an allergic response.

In some people, the immune system also reacts to particular foods. The first time an allergen is eaten, it is detected by the immune system. This reacts by producing a chemical called **IgE**. The IgE circulates in the blood and attaches itself to the surface of special white blood cells called mast cells. You don't notice anything happening at this stage. Whenever you eat that food in the future, though, the allergen in the food interacts with the IgE. This makes the mast cells release **histamine** and other chemicals. As these chemicals circulate in the blood, they cause the symptoms of the allergic response.

WHAT ARE THE SYMPTOMS OF AN ALLERGIC RESPONSE?

These vary from one person to another. Some occur within minutes of eating the food while others may take several hours to develop. The symptoms often include:

- tingling lips, tongue, mouth, and throat
- vomiting and diarrhoea
- skin rash, itching, and eczema
- asthma and other breathing difficulties.

Mild allergic reactions can usually be treated with anti-histamines.

ANAPHYLAXIS

This is a severe type of allergic reaction which can be life-threatening. The symptoms are similar to those of an ordinary allergy, but are much more severe. Swelling in the throat can prevent normal breathing and reduced blood pressure can lead to weakness and collapse. **Anaphylaxis** is usually treated with a medicine called **adrenalin** (also known as epinephrine). People known to be at risk from an anaphylactic reaction should always carry this medicine with them, and know how to use it.

Food intolerances and food aversions

Food intolerances are similar to allergic reactions, but the immune system is not thought to be involved. Symptoms are usually slower to appear and are rarely life-threatening. Some food intolerances are caused by an inability of the digestive system to process particular foods. For example, some people have an intolerance to **lactose**, a sugar in milk.

Food aversions may cause the same symptoms as food allergies and intolerances. However, there is no physical basis for the reaction – it is simply the result of a person being convinced that a certain food will cause their body to react in a particular way.

HOW CAN YOU TELL IF YOU HAVE AN ALLERGY?

Some people think they may have a food allergy because they know they feel unwell after eating a particular food. This can be a first step to finding out what they are allergic to. However, as many foods are a mixture of substances, more precise information is needed.

Keeping a food diary can be a good start in identifying the foods to which a person is allergic. This means writing down everything they eat and drink each day. They also keep a record of any symptoms and when they happen. Looking back over a period of several weeks can help show whether there is a link between their symptoms and certain foods.

ELIMINATION DIETS

This was one of the first ways for diagnosing an allergy. They are less common now as they are time-consuming, expensive, and provide poor nutrition. Elimination diets should always be overseen by a doctor. At the beginning, only a very limited number of foods are allowed. These are chosen from foods that are least likely to provoke an allergic response. Another food is then introduced and symptoms monitored again. If there is no allergic response, another food is reintroduced. This process continues until an allergic response is triggered. This identifies the last food tested as an allergen for that person.

BLOOD TESTS

These can be done when skin tests are not possible, for example, if a patient is likely to suffer a severe reaction, has a skin condition such as eczema, or is on medication that would affect the results. A blood sample is tested against a range of allergens to see whether it contains IgE to those allergens. Blood tests like these are known as RAST (Radioallergosorbent test). Other types of blood test can also be carried out, such as ELISA (enzyme-linked immunosorbent assay). However, results from blood tests may not always be accurate.

DBPCFC TEST

These letters stand for Double Blind Placebo Controlled Food Challenge. This is thought to be the most accurate way to test for food allergies, but must only be done in hospital. The suspected allergen is added to a patient's food without their knowledge. The patient is then monitored to see if there is a reaction to it. Like the blood tests, this type of testing eliminates any possibility of the patient's mind affecting the body's reaction.

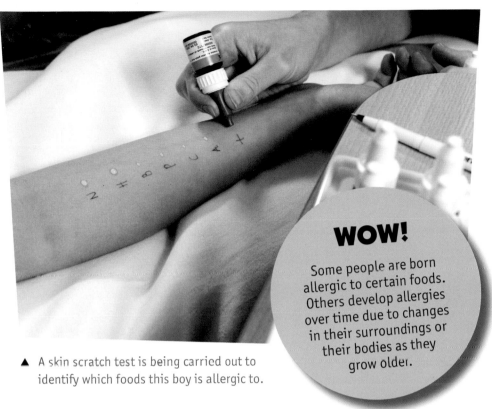

▲ A skin scratch test is being carried out to identify which foods this boy is allergic to.

SKIN SCRATCH TEST

A drop of an extract from a food is applied to the skin, either via a tiny scratch or pinprick. Using a series of scratches or pinpricks, a range of different food extracts can be tested. The picture on the cover of this book shows a skin test. Each patch contains a small amount of a different allergen. An allergy can sometimes be identified by looking at the skin responses.

If a person is allergic to a food, their skin will react to it, turning red and sometimes swelling. If the skin does not react, they are unlikely to be allergic to the food that was applied there. However, skin tests are not always accurate. They are better at indicating which foods a person is not allergic to than identifying those they are allergic to. Never try to do this sort of testing yourself – you could suffer a dangerous reaction!

OTHER ALLERGY TESTS

All the above methods for diagnosing allergies are based on scientific evidence. However, advertisements often appear in magazines, newspapers, health food shops, and other places offering other ways of testing for allergies. Some of these offers are very expensive, and many are not based on any scientific evidence at all.

FOOD ALLERGIES
– some common allergies

There is a wide range of foods that can trigger an allergic response, but some foods are found to do this more commonly. Others do it rarely. Some people are allergic to just a single food, others are allergic to a few foods, and some are allergic to many.

CHILDREN AND FOOD ALLERGIES

Some children are born with food allergies. In others, allergies develop over a period of time. The most common foods to which children are allergic include:

- eggs
- peanuts
- cows' milk
- soya
- wheat.

These allergies often become less severe as the child grows up, and in many cases they disappear completely.

ADULTS AND FOOD ALLERGIES

Adults tend to be allergic to a different range of foods from children. Foods that commonly cause allergies in adults include:

- shellfish such as crab, prawns, lobster, and shrimps
- nuts including peanuts, walnuts, brazil nuts, and almonds
- eggs
- yeast.

▲ Each of these foods can cause allergic reactions in some people.

Research shows that some allergies, including food allergies, are inherited. Although this does not necessarily mean that all members of a family are allergic to the same food, it does mean that some families seem to have a higher incidence of allergy problems (such as hay fever, asthma, and eczema).

AVOIDING ALLERGENS

Governments have recognised that food allergies can be serious. In the USA, it is estimated that over 4 million people have a food allergy! To make it easier for people to avoid eating foods that they are

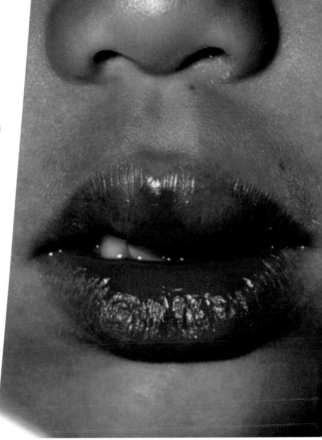

▲ This boy has a peanut allergy. His lip has swollen as a result of eating peanuts.

allergic to, many countries now have strict food labelling rules. These mean that all the ingredients in a food must be listed on the packaging. There must also be clear warnings if any of the common allergens are included. They are gluten, shellfish, eggs, fish, peanuts, nuts, soybeans, milk, celery, mustard, sesame, and sulphur dioxide.

Many companies also now produce foods that can be used in place of those that might cause an allergic reaction. For example, egg-free cakes can be eaten by people with an allergy to eggs.

Vaccines for food allergies?

Scientists are trying to develop vaccines that would prevent the immune system from responding to allergens in foods. These would be especially useful for people likely to suffer severe reactions to allergens such as peanuts and wheat. Although research is still at an early stage, scientists hope that a vaccine may soon be available for testing in humans.

▲ Wheat is used to make many everyday foods. People with a wheat allergy have to avoid these.

NO BREAD OR MILK?

Two common foods that cause allergic reactions are wheat and cows' milk. These might seem easy to exclude from the diet, but they are often hidden in foods where you may not expect to find them!

Wheat is the cereal grain that is ground to make most of our flour. This is then used to make many different foods, such as breads, cakes, biscuits, and pasta. People who are allergic to wheat cannot eat anything containing wheat flour. Instead, they can use flour made from other grains, such as rice and corn, or from other sources such as potato starch and soya. A mixture of one or more of these flours often produces better results than using a single one alone. The quantity of flour may need to be changed when using these flours in recipes written for wheat flour.

HIDDEN WHEAT!

Wheat flour can be found in some unlikely foods. These include hot dogs, sausages, chocolate drinks, and even some ice creams.

GLUTEN FREE SOLUTION?

One of the main allergens in wheat is gliadin, which is part of the protein, gluten. Many people with a wheat allergy are told to follow a gluten-free diet. However, not all gluten-free foods are suitable for all people with wheat allergies. Some people are allergic to other parts of the wheat grain. These gluten-free foods may still contain other parts of the wheat grain.

MILK ALLERGY

One of the most common childhood allergies is to cows' milk. There are several different proteins in the whole milk, the curds, and the whey, any of which may cause an allergic reaction. Sheep milk and goats' milk can be good substitutes for cows' milk for some adults. However, as they contain some proteins similar to those in cows' milk, they may not be suitable for everybody, especially children. Milk-like products made from rice and soya are also available and can be used in place of animal milks by some people with a milk allergy.

People who are allergic to milk also need to avoid other dairy products such as cheese, butter, yoghurt, and cream. In home cooking, you can often use water instead of milk. Cows' milk is used in many other foods, though, and it may not always be obvious! Many processed foods and factory-made cakes, snacks, and biscuits contain dried milk.

▲ Foods like these are made from milk. Some people are allergic to them, and some may not be able to digest the lactose these products contain.

Lactose intolerance

✔ Lactose intolerance is often thought of as a milk allergy but it is quite different. Lactose is a sugar found in animal milks.

✔ In humans, an enzyme called lactase is needed to digest lactose. Some people have too little lactase and therefore cannot digest lactose.

✔ Drinking milk and eating milk products can cause symptoms such as diarrhoea because of the undigested lactose. This is called lactose intolerance.

WHAT ARE NUT, FISH, AND SHELLFISH ALLERGIES?

Some allergies can be very confusing! Many people associate an allergy to nuts with peanuts — but peanuts are not really nuts at all! People with fish allergies can often eat shellfish without any ill effects. While others can eat fish, but not shellfish!

NUT ALLERGY

A nut allergy actually means an allergy to tree nuts. These are nuts such as walnuts, hazelnuts, almonds, pecans, Brazils, macadamias, and cashews. People who are allergic to nuts like these will also be allergic to foods containing any products made from them. These include nut oils, sweets such as praline, marzipan, and nougat, and some sauces and pesto. Tree nuts can also be found in mueslis, breakfast cereals, and health bars.

PEANUT ALLERGY

Although they are called nuts, peanuts are actually from the same plant family as peas and beans! They grow underground and are also called ground nuts and monkey nuts. People who are allergic to peanuts are often not allergic to tree nuts. They may, however, be allergic to other things from the bean family, such as soya, green beans, and kidney beans. Peanut products are not always obvious on food labels. They can be hidden in phrases like "hydrolysed vegetable protein". Sometimes people are allergic to nuts and peanuts.

Look out for nuts and peanuts!

Many foods that are made in factories may not contain nuts or peanuts themselves. However, they may contain traces of nuts from other foods that are made there. Foods made in factories that use nuts often have a warning label.

▶ These may look like an ordinary nut snack, but they are actually made from soya beans. They can be safely eaten by people with nut allergies – as long as they are not also allergic to soya!

▲ This girl has a serious allergy so she wears a medi-bracelet. It tells medical workers how to treat her if she suffers a severe allergic reaction.

FISH ALLERGIES

Although we often think of them together, fish and shellfish are very different. A fish allergy actually means an allergy to fish such as cod, salmon, trout, sardine, tuna, and halibut. People who are allergic to a particular type of fish may also react badly to other types of fish. This is because they often contain many similar allergens.

SHELLFISH ALLERGIES

Shellfish are not actually fish at all! They belong to two groups of sea and freshwater creatures, called:

- crustaceans – such as shrimps, crabs, and lobsters
- molluscs – such as oysters, mussels, cockles, and whelks.

As with fish allergies, being allergic to one type of shellfish may mean you will react badly to others, too. Some people are allergic to crustaceans, others to molluscs, and some to both.

Look out for fish and shellfish!

Many processed foods such as some meat substitutes and hot dogs contain hidden fish and shellfish. Oriental dishes commonly use fish and shellfish products for flavouring and thickening. Some fish parts are even used for surprising things such as some wine-making and coffee-making processes!

▲ If your doctor thinks you might have a food allergy, he or she will probably send you to see a doctor who specializes in allergies.

WHAT'S IT LIKE LIVING WITH FOOD ALLERGIES?

Ewan and Jamie are two normal, healthy teenagers. They live life to the full, enjoying almost everything that other teenagers do. They share one problem, though – they both have a food allergy.

EWAN'S STORY

My parents first found out I had a food allergy when I was about a year and a half old. I choked and held my throat and my face went very pale. Mum and Dad watched me carefully after I'd been very sick, until the symptoms had passed. They took me to see a dietitian, who suggested I should stay away from all the foods that affected me.

Now I know I need to avoid peanuts, pulses, lentils, and peas – and any foods that might have these in them, like oils. It's alright at home, but I have to be very careful if I eat out anywhere. If I do accidentally eat one of the foods I'm allergic to, my mouth waters a lot and my lips feel as if they've been burnt. My throat swells up and then I'm very sick. I don't need any medicine for my allergy, but I do have to be really careful. One of the worst things – apart from it feeling so awful – is that I can't eat some foods that my friends say taste really nice.

JAMIE'S STORY

When did your parents first realise you might have a food allergy?
When I was about nine months old, I had an allergic reaction to a fruit and nut bar. My face swelled up and my whole body turned bright crimson! They called the doctor and I was sent straight to hospital.

What did the hospital do or suggest?
They treated me for that reaction and then kept me in overnight. Later, we went back for a controlled challenge test and that proved I had an allergy.

What effect did this have on your life?
It meant that I couldn't eat some foods. It also singled me out as unequal because we have to tell someone wherever I go.

What do you have to be careful about now?
Everything I eat! I have to check the ingredients on everything. I can't eat any foods that could have even the tiniest bit of nut in – I even have to check about shampoos, oils, and anything else that can go on my body!

Do you carry any medicines for your allergy?
Yes, an **epipen®**. I have to stab it in my thigh if I start to have breathing difficulties. If I collapse, someone else has to do this for me.

How do other people respond to your allergy?
Most of my friends are OK about it. One time I was on a camp trip and a boy kept teasing me about it. That made me feel really down. It's not my fault I have an allergy.

As you can see from these two case studies, food allergies can be very different. Some, like Ewan's, cover a wide range of foods. Others, like Jamie's, are very specific. Some, like Ewan's, produce unpleasant but not life-threatening effects and do not need medical treatment. Others, like Jamie's, can be extremely serious and need prompt treatment with the right medicine.

A study in the UK found that 15 per cent of 11-year-olds and 19 per cent of 15-year-olds avoided certain foods because they thought they could not tolerate them, but only 2 per cent were found to have a real allergy or intolerance. While food allergies must be taken seriously, you need to first make sure that you do have an allergy before you start cutting different foods from your diet. Visit your doctor to discuss any concerns you have.

FOOD ADDITIVES ?
– what is added and why

Just about anything added to food is a food additive! The term is usually used to mean a range of special chemicals commonly added to foods to change the colour, flavour, texture, or storage properties.

Food additives are not new. Different things have been added to foods for hundreds of years. For example, meat and fish have been salted to preserve them. Vegetables have been pickled in vinegar, and herbs and spices have been used to add flavours. Salt, vinegar, herbs, and spices are all therefore examples of natural food additives. When we talk about food additives, though, we usually mean artificial additives made from chemicals rather than natural sources.

LABELLING FOOD ADDITIVES

To make sure all our foods and drinks are safe, there are strict regulations about what may be added. Chemicals must be tested to make sure they are not dangerous in any way. Then they are given an identifying code, name, or number that must appear on the food packaging. This makes sure that when you buy the food, you know exactly what is in it.

▲ The rules governing the use and labelling of food additives are different in different countries.

CONTROLLING HOW ADDITIVES ARE USED

In the UK, foods are regulated by the Foods Standards Agency (FSA) and are also subject to EU laws. In the United States, the Food and Drug Administration (FDA) regulates foods.

Throughout Europe, food additives are given E numbers. In the European Union, food additives may only be used if:

* there is a technological need for their use
* they do not mislead the consumer
* they present no hazard to the health of the consumer.

In the United States, colourings have to be labelled with a F D & C (Food, Drug, and Cosmetic) number. Food labels in the United States must also show the reason why an additive that acts as a preservative has been used. For example, "to protect flavour" or "mould inhibitor".

The six main groups of food additives each has a different purpose:

What do food additives do?

type of additive	reason for use	examples
antioxidants	stop foods containing fats and oils tasting "off"	ascorbic acid E300
colourings	alter the colour of the food	cucurmin E100 – yellow
emulsifiers, stabilisers, gelling agents, and thickeners	alter the texture of the food and prevent ingredients separating	pectin E 440 – sets jams
flavourings and flavour enhancers	bring out the natural flavours of the food	monosodium glutamate E621
preservatives	stop food going bad	sulphur dioxide E220
sweeteners	make the food sweeter	saccharin E954

Fluoride and drinking water

✔ Fluoride is a chemical that occurs naturally in very small amounts in water. Dental research has shown that higher amounts of fluoride can help to prevent tooth decay.

✔ In some places, fluoride is added to drinking water at water treatment centres. This means that everybody automatically gets a dose of extra fluoride.

✔ People have argued for years about this. Some say it is good, because it will reduce tooth decay. Others say it is wrong because people are being forced to drink a food additive. There is no simple solution – what do you think?

WHY ARE SOME PEOPLE WORRIED ABOUT FOOD ADDITIVES?

Food additives might do all sorts of good things to your food – make it look better, taste better, or stop it going bad – but many people are worried about other possible effects additives have on human health and behaviour.

The problem is, nobody really knows the effects of food additives yet. There are many scientific studies looking at the effects of food additives on human health. If a study indicates that a particular additive could harm our health in some way, the additive is usually banned from our foods. We sometimes hear big scare stories about additives that have been shown to cause serious diseases, such as cancer. Governments usually react very quickly to remove all foods that contain such additives.

FOOD ADDITIVES AND BEHAVIOUR

Many scientific studies have been carried out to find out whether there is a link between food additives, (particularly some colourings), and hyperactivity, ADHD, and other behavioural problems in children. However, there is not a clear-cut answer to this: some studies have shown a link, while others have shown the opposite. Many parents think it best to be cautious and avoid such additives in their young children's diets.

▼ Sweets often contain many different additives. In the 1970s, many sweet manufacturers changed their red coloured sweets to another colour because of health concerns about the red dye amaranth.

FOOD ADDITIVES, ALLERGIES, AND INTOLERANCES

In some people, a particular food additive causes an allergic reaction, or aggravates another condition. In people who already suffer from asthma or eczema, eating a particular additive may make the condition worse.

Other people find a particular food additive causes a reaction such as a skin rash or runny nose. When people know they have an allergy, or reaction to a particular additive, they usually try to avoid foods containing it.

NOT NATURAL?

Some people avoid food additives because they feel they are not natural. They are concerned about eating artificial chemicals. They worry about what effects those chemicals may have on their body. However, other people think that it does not matter because all our foods are just a mixture of chemicals such as sugars, proteins, and fats.

The main objection to additives seems to be that they are artificial, created in laboratories, or made from things that we would not normally eat. For example, tartrazine is made from coal tar. Another major objection is that we don't know the long-term effects of eating a combination of many different artificial additives.

Not all food additives are artificial, though. For example, pectin is found naturally in some fruits, but can be added to others to make them set into jams and jellies.

Cochineal is an expensive bright red dye that comes from the cochineal insect. The insect is from South America and Mexico and lives on cacti. It produces a type of acid to scare away other insects. This acid can be taken from the insect's body and eggs to make the dye called cochineal, which is used as a food colouring. After artificial dyes were invented in the late 1800s, the insect wasn't used as much anymore. However, new health concerns about artificial food additives have made cochineal dyes popular once more. The increased demand has resulted in people cultivating the insect again.

Healthy eating is a matter of educating yourself about different foods – what is in them and where they come from. You also need to know which foods make you feel well and which do not. Then you need to decide to make healthy food choices.

SPECIAL RECIPES

People with allergies or food intolerances or who follow special diets often need special recipes. These recipes help them avoid the ingredients that they are allergic or sensitive to. There are tasty alternatives to all kinds of foods. For example, fresh or dried fruit can be used instead of adding sugar.

Planning meals, choosing the right recipes, and adapting recipes can be especially helpful. Taking time with shopping and reading food labels means that people who follow special diets can choose foods carefully. Planning in advance means that they will be able to eat healthily and still have an interesting and varied diet – without compromising their safety.

Remember these basic food hygiene and safety rules whenever you prepare food:

✔ always wash your hands before you begin;

✔ make sure work surfaces and utensils are clean;

✔ take care when using knives and other sharp utensils;

✔ check with an adult before using the cooker.

Be helpful – leave the kitchen clean and tidy when you finish!

▼ Bean and pasta soup

BEAN AND PASTA SOUP

This soup provides a balanced meal that can be enjoyed by most healthy people. It is low in saturated fat and is therefore suitable for people who wish to reduce their intake of saturated fats. It is also suitable for people who are vegetarians. Beans are a good protein source for people who do not eat meat.

The recipe makes enough for two people. For one person, use half of each quantity. For four people, double each quantity.

Ingredients:
1 tablespoon olive oil (or vegetable oil such as sunflower oil)
$1/2$ onion
$1/2$ carrot
$1/2$ celery stick
200 g (7 oz) tin chopped tomatoes
50 g (1.75 oz) small pasta shapes
200 g (7 oz) tin canellini beans (or other beans), drained
1 teaspoon mixed herbs
1 vegetable stock cube

Method:
First, prepare the vegetable stock by crumbling the stock cube into 500 ml (1 pint) boiling water. Stir until dissolved then leave to stand.

Then prepare the soup:
Finely chop the onion, carrot, and celery.
Heat the oil in a large saucepan.
Add the chopped vegetables and stir fry until softened.
Add tinned tomatoes and stir well.
Add stock and bring to the boil.
Add pasta shapes. Bring back to the boil.
Turn the heat down and simmer gently for 5 minutes, stirring occasionally.
Add beans. Simmer for 2–3 minutes, or until the pasta is tender.

Serve in bowls. For a special look, float a sprig of fresh parsley or basil on top of each bowl.

APPLE FLAPJACKS

People who are allergic to wheat need to eat a wheat-free diet. People with coeliac disease must avoid foods that contain gluten, which is present in cereals such as wheat, rye, and barley. However, some can include a small amount of pure oats in their diet. This recipe does not include wheat or gluten. It is therefore suitable for people with a wheat allergy or coeliac disease, as well as for most other people.

Ingredients:
2 large bramley apples,
   peeled, cored, and sliced
juice of $\frac{1}{2}$ lemon
150 g (5 oz) butter
75 g (3 oz) brown sugar
75 g (3 oz) golden syrup
225 g (8 oz) rolled oats
$\frac{1}{2}$ teaspoon ground cinnamon
a pinch of salt

Method:
Preheat the oven to 190°C
(375°F), Gas mark 5. Place the
apples in a small saucepan
together with the lemon juice
and a little water. Bring to the
boil, cover and simmer for 10
minutes or until the apple is
soft, then mash the apple to a
soft purée.

▲ Apple flapjacks

Melt the butter, sugar, and syrup in another saucepan, but do not let the mixture boil. Stir in the oats, cinnamon, and salt and mix well.

Press half the mixture into a 20 cm (8 inch) sandwich tin. Spread the apple purée on top, then cover with the remaining flapjack mixture. Bake for 25 minutes, or until golden brown.

Remove from the oven and mark into slices, but leave to cool before attempting to remove from the tin.

STRAWBERRY SMOOTHIE

People who are allergic to milk, or who are lactose-intolerant, need to eat a milk-free diet. Not only must they avoid milk, they must also avoid all foods made from milk, such as butter, cheese, and yoghurt. However, some products are available that can be used instead of cows' milk. This recipe uses milk made from soya beans instead of cows' milk. It is therefore suitable for people with a milk allergy or lactose-intolerance, as well as for most healthy people.

Ingredients:
1 vanilla soya yoghurt
6 strawberries
2 ice cubes
2 teaspoons vanilla extract

Method:
Blend all ingredients in a blender until smooth. (Take care – you may need help from an adult when using the blender.)
You could use other types of fruit such as raspberries or bananas instead of strawberries. It could also be made with frozen fruit.

► Strawberry smoothie

GLOSSARY

adrenalin (epinephrine) medicine used to treat severe allergic reactions

allergen substance (a protein) that produces an allergic response

allergic will react to an allergen

anaemia shortage of red blood cells due to a shortage of iron. Anaemia can cause weakness, breathlessness, and low energy.

anaphylaxis severe allergic response

antioxidant one of several chemicals found in some foods that may help to prevent illnesses

arthritis disorder where the joints become inflamed. A joint is where two different bones meet, such as the ankle or wrist.

asthma condition that affects breathing

balanced diet diet with the right amounts of different kinds of foods

calorie unit of energy, one thousandth of a kilocalorie

carbohydrate nutrient, such as sugar or starch, that provides energy

cereal grain seeds from cereal plants such as maize, wheat, or rice

cholesterol type of fat found in meat and animal products

coeliac disease condition in which the sufferer is sensitive to gluten

constipation condition where faeces are dry and hard

dehydration having too little water

diabetes condition in which the body's control of blood sugar levels does not function properly

diarrhoea condition where faeces are semi-liquid

dietitian person qualified in nutrition and dietary matters

digestive system the organs that digest food

eczema condition in which the skin becomes dry, flaky, and itchy

epipen® injection of adrenalin (epinephrine) used during a life-threatening allergic reaction. It stops the throat swelling and the blood pressure falling too low, ensuring that the heart keeps beating.

fibre substance in plants that cannot be digested, but which helps people digest food

folic acid vitamin needed for healthy development before birth

free range animals that are not kept in cages

glucagon hormone involved in controlling blood sugar level

gluten protein found in wheat and some other grains

halal meat meat from animals slaughtered according to Muslim law

histamine chemical released during allergic reaction. This can be blocked by a chemical called an anti-histamine.

hormone natural substance that regulates bodily processes

IgE chemical produced by the immune system in response to an allergen

immune system the body's defence system

inflammation area of the body which is hot, red, swollen, and painful

insulin hormone involved in controlling blood sugar level

intestine part of the digestive system

kosher food prepared according to Jewish dietary law

lactose sugar found in milk

malabsorption not absorbed fully

microbes organisms too small to be seen by the naked eye

migraine severe headache often accompanied by sickness and other symptoms

minerals chemicals that are found naturally on Earth

nutrients parts of food that the body can use

nutrition to do with nutrients

obesity the state of being so overweight that health is at risk

protein nutrient needed for growing and repairing damage

saturated fats fats found in meat and animal products

spina bifida condition that affects the spinal cord

ulcerated when the skin or mucus membrane, of the stomach lining for example, becomes covered in open sores that form pus. The surrounding tissue starts to die.

unsaturated fat fat that has few hydrogen atoms

vitamin chemical needed in small amounts for health

FINDING OUT MORE

You can find out a lot more about healthy food choices, special diets, and allergies from books, encyclopaedias, and websites.

BOOKS

Allergy Information for Teens, Karen Bellenir ed. (Omnigraphics, Inc, 2006)

Body Needs: titles include *Vitamins and minerals for a healthy body, Carbohydrates for a healthy body, Fats for a healthy body,* and *Water and fibre for a healthy body,* (Heinemann Library, 2003). This series looks at what the human body needs to function healthily.

Eating for Health: Titles include *Low Cholesterol Cooking, High vitality, Allergy-free cooking, Cooking for Diabetes, Gluten-free Cooking,* and *Vegan cooking* (Raintree, 2004)

It Happened to Me: Diabetes, Katherine Moran (Scarecrow Press, 2004)

Need to Know: Asthma, Steve Parker (Heinemann Library, 2004)

Penguin Companion to Food, Alan Davidson (Penguin, 2002)

Teen Issues: Diet, Joanna Kedge and Joanna Watson (Raintree, 2004)

Understanding Ingredients, Anne Barnett (Heinemann Library, 1998)

WEBSITES

www.defra.gov.uk

UK Department for Environment, Food and Rural Affairs (Defra) aims to "work for the essentials of life – food, air, land, water, people, animals, and plants".

www.food.gov.uk

The main website of the Food Standards Agency (FSA), an independent UK government department. It provides allergy information for caterers.

www.eatwell.gov.uk

An FSA website that provides consumer advice and information on healthy eating. It also provides information about food allergies.

www.foodtech.org.uk

A site for students and teachers on food technology.

www.coolfoodplanet.org

Food fun for young people from the European Food Information Council.

www.lifebytes.gov.uk

LifeBytes gives facts about food and all other aspects of health for young people aged 11–14.

www.foodstandards.gov.au

Food labels differ around the world; this site contains useful information about food labels from Australia and New Zealand.

www.allergy.org.uk/food_allergy

Learn more about food intolerance and allergies.

www.allergyuk.org/

Allergy UK is a national medical charity dealing with allergy. They provide up-to-date information on all aspects of allergy, food intolerance, and chemical sensitivity.

WHY NOT LOOK UP MORE ABOUT THESE TOPICS?

- the digestive system
- the immune system
- working in polar regions
- living in space
- allergy research.

INDEX